Brother and Sister Act

Companion Poems

Brother and Sister Act

Companion Poems

by

Mimi Moriarty

&

Frank Desiderio

Cover image by Ellie Murphy
Author photo by Matthew Desiderio

ISBN: 979-8-90146-915-6
Library of Congress Control Number: 2026939308

Kelsay Books
502 South 1040 East, A-119
American Fork, Utah 84003
Kelsaybooks.com

We dedicate this work to our family who loves, inspires, and sustains us.

Acknowledgments

Thank you to the following publications, in which versions of these poems previously appeared:

Amethyst Review: "The First Tree"

Holy Poetry on Substack: "Return of the Jedi," "Prayer After the Fire"

Rensselaerville, NY Library Poem-A-Day for National Poetry Month: "Watching the Turkey"

Writers Almanac Poetry Contest: "Seventy and Drawing Energy"

Contents

These poems are arranged as companion poems, each set reflecting a particular theme or image. They were written separately by two siblings and paired specifically for this manuscript.

The first of the set, written by Mimi Moriarty, is in standard type, and the second of the set, written by Frank Desiderio, is in italics.

FAMILY

SEASONS

FRAILTIES

FAMILY

Recipes: A Litany

In her modest penmanship
my grandmother lays down delicate ribbons
line by line instructions for the sauce

she breaks them up into scenes
        the garden where you pick the basil
        the basement where you can tomatoes
        the kitchen chair over which
        you hang the homemade pasta
each location made holy by the child as witness

I flip through her stained cards as litany:

Blessed be the Almond Paste Cookies
Blessed be the Fried Dough
Blessed be the Artichokes Dipped in Butter
        the Crab Cakes Served with Tartar Sauce
Blessed be the Eggplant, Slice Thin, Fry Lightly
Blessed be the Ricotta Pie from Grace Martino
        the Cannoli, Dust with Powdered Sugar
        the Turkey Dressing with Chestnuts
        the Greens and Beans, Wash Thoroughly
        the Clam Chowder with the Secret Ingredient!
Blessed be the Sauce
Blessed be the Sauce
Blessed be the Sunday Sauce Bubbling on the Stove

St. Linoleum, hold me up
St. Amana, cool me down
St. BAB-O, cleanse me

St. Can of Campbell's Tomato Soup, comfort me
St. Overflowing Pantry, sustain me
St. Aloe Plant in the Corner, heal me
St. Rusted Recipe Box, never let me forget:

she slaps the dough on a board
        In the name of the Father
she splits chicken breasts with a cleaver
        And of the Son
she peels yellow onions layer by layer
        And of the Holy Spirit
she rubs garlic in her palm until it becomes a paste—Amen!

The Christmas Baccala

The Christmas baccala
is as hard as a board
and as far from fresh
as Christmas is from cod fishing.

In a Philly basement
it goes into a pot to soak
and drain off the salt.
The pot is a slow-flowing fountain
created by a dripping faucet
that overflows overnight and
all the next day.

Drawn out and drained
and cut into cubes
It goes into the broth
with olives, celery and potatoes

to become the first course
in the Feast of the Seven Fishes.
The baby says, "Papa,
leave some Pesce Stocco
for Santa Clause."

Expectations of My Grandmother

Outside, the thermometer under an icicle,
cousins arrive down the slippery path,
they know what Sunday means:
pizza in deep pans scattered with oregano.

She rises from the table on her scrawny legs
heads toward the basement steps, the pantry
cool, glistening with summer tomatoes,
her vocabulary tangled in two languages.

Thumps down, thumps up, she transforms
the kitchen into a factory of under-aged
apprentices, we all take our turn at kneading,
sprinkling, oiling, washing, putting away.

She glances at the clock before it coo-coos,
hangs her apron like a wreath on spindles,
turns up the radio, we listen: Verdi,
Rossini, Puccini sung by Mario Lanza.

She Had Forearms Like Popeye

Her father said she was stronger than death
her first three siblings slain by the Spanish Flu.
She cleaned her house with a vengeance
scoured as if the flu virus was on every surface.

She loved her grandkids stronger than death
scrubbed us with a rough washcloth
threatened us with her wooden spoon
to make sure we kept everything pristine.

She had forearms like Popeye from punching
the pizza dough, kneading it as if it
needed to be pounded into submission,
throwing up clouds of flour whiter than white.

She baked her potting soil to kill germs
bleached her sheets threadbare
used her electric vacuum like a rug beater
pounding the dirt out of the carpet.

At age ninety she had a quadruple bypass.
She tried to bypass death but it weakened her.
On her death bed she sat bolt upright and spit.
She spat in the face of death with her last breath.

His Hammer

An old hammer turned in his hand
the wood smoothed from the grip of his fist
the head bound for a loud smack, rat-a-tat-tat

I am sitting on the basement's bottom step
mooning over my father's form
a god in overalls splattered with paint

I still remember the scent of wood being cut
the sound of wood being pounded, coerced
into practical things for the upstairs tableau.

I roam in the wreckage of my own basement
admitting defeat as I rummage through junk
and hunt through tattered boxes, looking for

anything valuable or redeemable that will
somehow lurch from the back of the closet
to the palm of my hand, something

as precious as his weathered hammer
to bookmark a memory, to stammer a new verse,
to sand into shape a woman's view of men

who make beautiful things, a woman who watches
in awe the humble sawdust, the sharp blade,
the lacquered act of creation.

My Dad's Good Hammer

Not the one with the frayed black electrician's tape
wrapped around the crack in the handle
but the lighter one, the one with the hickory handle,
unblemished but for the patina of work,
darkened and polished by oil from my dad's hand.

Now it sits, years after his death
on the side table with the magazine V built into it
that sat next to my dad's TV chair,
that sat next to his dad's reading chair,
that sat next to my lounge chair,
that is now in my brother's unfinished library
where I slept last night.

This morning, my brother's wife coos to their baby,
he clatters pans, the sounds of breakfast.

Ode to My Unborn Niece

You are designed   to develop
    in a swamp feathery limbs
    eventually lashes
    and fingernails

You are designed   to inhale
    that first breath with a crack
    and an Amen, relatives will
    swarm around you in your
    earthly realm

You are designed   to mirror
    our habits and our expressions
    even the clothing with its collars
    and buttons, fabric spooling
    to cover you

You are designed   to repeat verses
    to repeat patterns, to apologize
    to acquiesce to a higher form
    whether it be parent or patron
    and later to rebel

You are designed   O Unborn Child
    no bigger than a kumquat
    to laugh at the luminous terrain
    the sun-broken sky

Return of the Jedi

It's movie night at my brother's house
after a dinner of my dad's favorite pasta,
the one they serve in Italy on St. Joseph's Day
with toasted breadcrumbs for sawdust.

Watching a simple story of good and evil
about the force that binds a family in a place
where the bad guy is announced by drums and
has rigged the game, but in the end is redeemed.

My little niece loves the tribe of teddy bears
with their forest tricks that save the heroes on the ground
while above the ancient duel between love and hate
is fought with the whoosh and sweep and clash of light.

My little Jedi uses me as a lounge chair
while she eats blueberries
and I tell her what the big words mean.
This may be the best night of my life.

Beach Cottage

Surrounded by a bracelet of high-end homes
our cottage, monastic in simplicity, pauses,
as if time flattened and left it a shrine.

It used to be a yellow joke, but now it is a kindness
as if the origin of family had once resided here.
In its frame my father added muscle and tempo

as he pounded ten-penny nails, that is what I hear now,
on the porch, not the taut joggers or the espresso
machine next door, I hear the creak

of rocking chairs, the crooked door squeaking,
there is bacon in an iron skillet, my grandfather
must be awake, the coo of doves calling me home.

Memories constrict and sometimes it's just scribble,
sometimes it's fog, but this morning as the fog
navigates the roads and highways, I return

to this cottage, a wide morning, my daughter
still asleep, the hydrangeas in early bloom,
I rise to put bacon in the skillet,

this is who I have become.

At the Beach House

After seasons away,
I'm wrapped in an afghan
made by my mother's hands.
The cars outside sound like surf,
the people on their bikes calling
like dolphins.

This is Delaware, not Florida,
where men think they are Birds
of Paradise and dress in red jackets
and white pants, even when it's not
close to Christmas.

This is Delaware, a company town,
with codes: dress, building, conduct.
When we first moved here, I was twelve.
There were rabbits in the wild hedge,
deer at dusk, a cloud of hopping frogs so thick
they sounded like a hailstorm hitting the car.

High school all-nighters,
the Friday night drive,
stolen beer, rants
and one-upsmanship,
an alcohol haze the next morning.

Now, the must is thick
in this back bedroom;
the smell is in my clothes.

Best to stay outside,
walk past the mini-mansions
displaced from the suburbs
toward the fresh breeze coming
off the ocean.

Driving by My Grandfather's Yard

The roses are gone, the yard is filled with toys.
Who dug up the pale pink blossoms and
the white fringed with yellow?

In 1958 my grandfather planted rows
of tomatoes, peppers, squash, the squash
grew long enough to resemble baseball bats.
Who ate the last squash with its striped skin?

Who cupped the last rose with a citrus tinge,
sniffed its sweet succor?
Who bought toys, arranged them
across the wide lawn?

The fence is new, but the roof over
the cellar entrance, gone, new windows,
new patio, where are the poppies, azaleas
with their orange hue? The plum tree,
the fig tree, dug up by the root.

I pan the yard, notice this sea change
on land, land as large as my childhood,
as deep as rich loam, as heavy as
the stone steps, bereft of all I knew.

If my grandfather had been in the car,
he would have approved the plastic toys
strewn in his back yard. "Good," he
would have said, "there is life in the old house."

My grandmother would have tsk-tsked,
wondered why they had left the toys in the dew.
My grandfather, haunting the garden, winking,
would have dug a patch to grow the squash.

But I am alone, drive slowly past,
a vigil for my grandfather's yard.

Let It Go

Straining and wet,
the fish slipped my grasp,
with a wave of the tail it dove away.
My grandfather, who had just showed me
how to bait the hook,
was disappointed for me,
my first catch lost.
"We won't eat that one today,
you'll get him next time."
But I knew, even then, let it go.

Bare Top

It
stands
in a corner
by the window
its sagging branches
waiting for my daughter
from Manhattan to travel
through rush hour and the evening's
throes, waiting for the inevitable appraisal,
the crass removal of low branches
and then one-by-one each ornament's story
told, the year we were married, the dog, the canary,
third grade, every year spiraling toward today, then a riff
on a piano, all talking at once, we focus
on chips, dip and football, no one notices the bare top,
the absent angel, its fairy tale mission to finish the job,
but really, are we ever finished, even after ornaments are
abandoned
in a dusty attic,
then labeled
"antique" and
passed down
to grandchildren.

Christmas Archive

A spruce green against the grim winter gray,
a forest scent to perfume a closed-in day.

Each year a fresh green stage for the pageant
of the family's archive of ornaments.

A red and gold angel blowing its horn.
The crayoned card hanging from yellow yarn.

The antique glass tube with a curlicue tip,
the years recorded by missing paint chips.

A friend's hand-painted wedding favor,
entwined rings and Together Forever.

A tuna can painted gold hold's Santa's portrait
cut from wrapping paper—a school project.

There is a St Lucy's candle halo
and a Guadalupe cameo.

A tiny leg lamp from A Christmas Story—
Ralphie's dad's major award—Fragile.

The great-great-grandparent's star on top,
the beacon to show strangers where to stop.

Two Grandmothers

The one I knew least is the one I resemble
the one I knew best, she walks with me still.

I console myself with old photographs
she is laughing or posing in her go-to-hell hat.

What would she think of me sitting in a chair
waiting for words to flick from this pen.

The one I knew best, every wrinkle and curl,
is the grandmother whose presence I feel every day.

But the other grandmother, the one I knew least,
has somehow emerged and taken over my body.

I surrender to this grandmother, asthmatic and wheezing
who spoke no English, who sat in a chair

her leg oozing from an open wound,
she misses her life and claims mine for her own.

My Grandfather Taught Me

My grandfather taught me how to sharpen
a dull knife. He used a file to smooth nicks
guided the blade against a grinding wheel
spinning not too fast so the friction
wouldn't steal the temper from the steel.
When sparks flew and the wheel got too hot,
I splashed water from an old coffee can.
The smell of burning metal and wet stone
filled the air in his basement grinders shop.

Then the carborundum held in his hand
the knife at just the perfect angle
against the flat, gray abrasive stone;
stroke after stroke, the knife pointed away
from his body, gliding above his fingers
each stroke pushing some grit in front of the blade.

Finally, for a fine edge, stroked on a strop
the slap of the blade on leather took
the steel whiskers from the wire edge.

Years of working in kitchens every day
sharpened every weekend, reduced his knives
to thin blades in an oversized handle.

When they were too worn down to take to work
he turned them into garden implements.
With a flick of the wrist, he pruned away
a dead branch, trimmed the roses for spring.

When he died, his knives, each one a prize,
were awarded to his son and grandsons,
his granddaughters and their children.
Mine is in a Bible, like a bookmark.
The handle, like St. Paul's sword hilt, protrudes
from the top of those conversion stories,
a reminder of what happens to me
when I get dull and need to stay keen.

Last Breath

She labored four nights, four days
before she sighed her final breath.
I felt my own lungs collapse, alone
but for the presence of my daughter.

At twenty-five, my only daughter
loved then lost her grandmother
while she herself lived apart
in a city fast asleep.

Four March nights, four March days
we spent inside. My daughter stood
by the window, decorated each pane
with fingerprints in fog.

My mother made those curtains
my father hung them waiting.
I remember the tap-tap-tap
of the hammer against the brads.

We knitted, we baked, we cleaned
my father's house, but at night
with my daughter curled beside me,
I held my mother, still as a curtain.

I am here, Mama. Her stubborn breath
shallow, we dared not leave her,
a vigil like the vigil for her mother
seven years before.

There's a secret to the art of waiting.
It's not in the eyes, it's in the breath.
We hold it, then release it, my daughter
and I together, jigsawed and spent.

I Saw Spring Come

I saw Spring come to Washington D.C.
It was an unplanned trip
one I dreaded my whole life.

The train from New York
descended through a snowstorm
a white blur outside the window.

My sister and I arrived at the same time
coming to our mother's bedside
to listen to her breathing.

That Thursday evening our family gathered for supper.
Friday was a day of sitting vigil
listening to the variations in her breath
not sure she could still hear us.

We celebrated Mass on a makeshift altar
at the foot of her bed
a crucifix in her line of vision.

The hospice nurse came
and patiently explained
what the change in breathing meant,
what to expect.
We knew. Into God's hands . . .

On Saturday, each long pause
between labored breaths
was like a question: is this the last one?

Lifelong friends came to say goodbye
feeling her head as if a fever would break
and she would be fine.

There was a lot of touching,
hugging, hand-holding, fingering beads.
The family stayed close around her
to ward off the chilly sorrow.

Very early Sunday she went
to where her eyes looked when
she looked past us.

Her final breath was like the others,
then stillness. That terrible moment,
is she . . .?

Tears and prayers—
the hospice nurse red-eyed but clear-headed,
the mortician who came had a shaving cut.

Everyone slowed by a thick compassion.
We waited until Ash Wednesday for the wake.
For three days we selected songs and readings
sorted through pictures and memories.

Thursday, the day of the funeral
was what the Irish call "a soft morning,"
there was a misty rain.

At the luncheon afterward
there was kindness and pasta salad
and awkward moments.

The community was a comforter
on a cold afternoon.
That weekend, winter gave up the ghost,
springtime slipped into place.
The transformation felt like dislocation.
People were unsure about this shift,
could we trust the sun?

At the airport people passed me
in short sleeved shirts,
their winter coats strapped to their bags.

This Card

You are bent over lavender in the garden in slippers,
your apron stained with tomatoes, your belly swollen
with my brother, sitting in the corner knitting, mending
my ripped hem, a tributary of memories flows through me

how you pressed cookies past midnight on Christmas Eve
and ate sauerkraut and apples from the pan. This card
I hold in my hand triggers the scene of first cousins
eating egg salad while you are carted to the crematorium.

I cannot bear this haunting every May when anonymous
hucksters entice me down the greeting card aisle in rows
like prickly hedges, like paper headstones, I read them
out of habit, fingering the slanted font, the scalloped edge.

Afghan

My voice didn't crack during my mother's eulogy until
I heard her brother sob. Uncle Nick, her only brother,
pulled my attention from the back row. Hard talks
are easier if you don't meet anyone's eyes.

When I saw him wiping his eyes, the thumb of his right hand
passing over his right eye and his index finger pressing over
his left eye, then
they came together to pinch the bridge of his nose as if that
would stop the tears.
He sparked the fuse of my grief.

Today is the anniversary of when we all gathered around her
bed
and my brother's girlfriend, a nurse, told us she was dead.

My oldest sister says she thinks about our mom every day,
that she still misses her. She uses mom's pizzelle iron every
Christmas
to make the wafer-thin anise cookies.
My mom's initials are in the center of the iron,
each confection a momento mori.

When my sister talks about our mom,
I want to hear what she says
to help conjure up my love.

My mother used the wooden spoon to stir the sauce on Sunday
and whack me whenever she thought necessary.
She made me stand up for myself when the boombox I saved
for
turned out to be a piece of junk. She drove to the store,
planted me in front of the manager,
and told me to tell him to give me my money back,
which I did with a choked voice.
One Monday I woke to her shouting, telling my father
that my new suit was on the floor. She was outraged about
wrinkles
and dirt and disrespect and laziness.

Every day of my adult life, I make a ritual
of making my bed. I listen to poetry
as I put in order the disheveled night,
create a work of art with sheets, spread, pillow
and the afghan that my mother crocheted for me.

I remember her love in the same way that
I sorted through the array of her Christmas cookies
to find my favorites. Her genuine, high cheekbone smile
when I came to visit, she in a house dress.
I'd pick oranges from the trees in their yard
and she would squeeze the juice for me in the morning.

For their 50th wedding anniversary we threw a hell of a party
and I gave them a blessing.

This morning, just like every morning,
I spread the afghan on my bed
and smoothed out the wrinkles.

SEASONS

Waiting for Spring

There was rain
and a strike of lightning

the turkey in the yard
scurried into the underbrush

I would have done the same
if not protected by this roof

that pounds with the rain
and then pellets of hail

people wait all winter for spring
then complain when

winter shakes loose
and spring clatters in

What a joy to watch
the comedy this produces

the heavy-handed season
giving way to its own weight

allowing his younger sister
to try her hand at growing things.

Springtime in New York

Not a Frank Sinatra song
but the end of a long
aggravating assault
of snowplows on asphalt.

Last week the tree limbs
wore their winter grim,
then tiny yellow-green tufts,
infant fists in the strong sun.

Then the tulips and daffodils,
forsythia and jonquils.
Visitors video squirrels
and buy dozens of bagels.

Tourists form rolling roadblocks
on all the midtown sidewalks,
the native New Yorkers pace,
stymied and a whispered curse.

In Central Park the sentries
of white weeping cherry trees
remembering a Shinto shrine
whisper something of the divine.

Not a Frank Sinatra song
but the season that sings us
out of hibernation
to remember resurrection.

Trees I Have Claimed

Two willows bookended my grandfather's garden
the sway of their long, limber arms
meant summer in full swing
picnics, bocce, cousins.

His plum tree and two figs
thrived under his green-thumb,
his love and sweat bestowed on the fruit
paralleled his affection.

I believed he grew these trees for us
just so we could taste a real fig,
ripe red pulp bursting through
green skin, or a fist-sized plum.

And now, the double-trunk oak
a memorial to my grandfather
too thick to embrace
the heft of our history.

I have learned from these trees
and their arching protection
to bend in the storm,
to give, and give, and give.

I claim these trees,
and christen them in the name
        of memory.
They have christened me
        Old Woman of Many Words.

The First Tree

The first tree I remember was a giant oak
behind my boyhood home,
the marker between the driveway and the garden.

When I was six, I jumped and hung on the lowest branch,
hopped up and down clinging to the spring of that branch
hoping that I had the weight to break it.

Our watchful neighbor, Mr. Ozales, stopped me.
He explained to me the tree was a living thing
and the same way I didn't want to be hurt it didn't want to be
hurt.

He showed me that the smallest twig at the tip of the branch
was like my finger, not to be broken.
He had escaped the Nazis, was an arborist in Latvia.

Now, every forest is my sanctuary,
every tree is my upright companion,
pillars of praise to created mercy,
the ground from which everything springs.

Spring Blessing

Come, Spring, I offer blessings
to all belated buds and leaves
an invocation to the restless sprouts
straddling seasons of frost and heat.

Blessings to the whisper of green growing,
and the hint of flowering beds,
the spasms of winter have turned over
Spring's daffodil blonde head.

Blessings to rain, rain, rain,
its patter music in the forest where
fairies shiver under mushrooms,
keeping their translucent wings dry.

And blessings to the frazzled elders
who dodge winter by traveling
south, they have returned,
claim no new thing but survival.

Never Leave Without a Blessing

Never leave without a blessing
and if your grandmother is gone
and your father is missing
beg the god of your understanding.

Hang an icon of an angel
on the inside of your front door
place it just above eye level,
as you leave beseech a blessing.

Never go without a blessing
behind, around, ahead of you
to ward off negative thinking
to open the welcoming door.

Not just a prayer of protection
but a way to worry with hope
to suffer without depression
to take strides and keep your balance.

Receive your blessing and listen,
below the alarms and sirens
you'll hear a reverberation,
your whispered name—"Borne by Love."

Once blessed you can face the beast,
best it and not be disfigured.
No matter what, at the very least,
you will know that you are loved.

Speaking to the River

May I take this occasion to speak to the river
its graceful weight an entry into the annals
        of all rivers
its shade fades from plum to slivers of gray

I glimpse at the silver containment within
        its walls
which makes me believe in Sirens
        cloaked in dusk
their never-ending beckoning

I shield myself for this is an eternal call
to love the river amidst the grief of
        ordinary days
how they stretch between belief and
a ceaseless gnawing that all is lost

O River, run your course, and in those
mighty twists and turns, release the great
sorrow of the earth
        and mine
until it condenses into mist, then cloud
then torrents of rain
        rain down

My First

My first river—Potomac
My first ocean—Atlantic
My first bay—Chesapeake
My first lake—George
I met each at a different age
and always assumed I'd live near water.

In middle age my office was Pacific-adjacent.
Summer days I gazed at dolphins
and watched beach volleyball with delight.
Winter evenings on my way to the car
the sunsets stopped me, arrested by
the forever of the Pacific at magic hour.

In my current age, my love is the Hudson.
I walk with her most days.
We meet at Riverside Park South,
she treats me to barges
and I complain about the geese.

Right now, I ride along the Hudson
on the train to Albany.
She, the mistress of American history;
Venus in springtime
a classroom in summer
vivid woods in the fall
in winter her shallows frozen.

Through the flurries I can see
the gray waves caught in ice
against the shadow of white snow.

Rafts of black ducks
amber waves of sedge,
low-lying layers of fog,
and old homes, perched for the view,
now part of the landscape.

I love waters of transport,
am attracted to the interconnected universe
of wet and fresh and always.

Lent

I

I've missed another Lent with its hidden cautions.
Preparing for death, I have learned to relent.
Divine foxes in the woods sniff open Spring.

Small pieces of Christ float throughout
as if history were a Book of Braille and I were
fingerless. The rust and scrape of old tomes,

the mighty message of salvation evaporates
with the morning dew. This is enough, I say,
this is enough for now.

II

The story woven into bitter sacrifice—
what a son will do for his father—
pierced hands, wounded side,

a divine mission, like the son of a marine
who wants to be an artist, but he enlists,
serves in the desert.

His father reprimands him upon his return:
"Enough!" "Not enough!"
so he laces his wine with courage,

his bread with bones. Every ivory
morning he works on his mission—to be a son,
to love his father. Still he fades, just as Jesus would

have faded but for the rolled away rock, the empty
cave. What a son will do to prove his fealty,
his azure love turning to deep purple at dusk.

Lent at Butchart Gardens

A postcard someone sent me long ago
promised Eden's array of color
but what I see is a grey rainy dawn
and a garden's winter undercarriage.

The trimmed twigs of rose bushes
marshaled in rank after rank
of formal order. Climbing vines,
stripped but for their thorns,
are fixed secure with hemp
along crossbeams that
someday will transfix devoted eyes.

There is a straining purpose
in the plants—you can feel them
wanting to wake and stretch.
In the tropics, Lent is just an idea,
but, where spring is a cellar, Lent is felt.

This is the kind of rough climate that kills
small things and causes the strong to grow weary.
In this fertile place of dependence, surrender
so that repair can grow into an annual prayer
for rebirth.

Easter Morning

Every Easter without fail
I am reminded of the unflinching
scenes of the Passion, Death
and Resurrection, looming stories
from my past locked in battle
with scientific certainties

truth as it is beheld disturbs
the waters, ripples lap to shore
carrying the wreckage of my creed,
I have succumbed to a new faith
unblemished in its simplicity
a mighty shift in belief

friend, do not rail at my latest
pronouncements, the tide
has risen, the tide has rested,
we are companions on this
journey of deeply-held
belief, and as Easter unfolds

I release all else—except hope
in the risen, hope in the rising sun,
rising every day to new life, until
that final day when rising is
a chore, no more, no more.

He's There

Rightly they asked, "Where is the risen Lord?
When we last saw Him He was surely dead."
Everyone had his own answer. John said
"The Word made flesh now resides in the word."
The mystic in her desert cave answered:
"If you want to find him then look inward."
Year after year, people still ask, "Where?"
In ordinary and out-of-body
exertions to give aid to the needy,
He is there.
In your care for the earth,
He is there.
In the healing that comes out of nowhere,
He is there.
Some beliefs I talk myself into
but other beliefs I just know to be true.

Seasons Turning

The foliage is cantankerous this year,
barbed leaves waving like the hands
of grandmothers to peepers passing by,
their undersides pocked with spores,
the edges curling, twisting on stems.

I'm in a cello mood. I listen to strings
against a bow, a motion few have
mastered, their shoulders sore
from months of practice, often
sounding like angry parrots
or bees circling. The lofty
strings rise from the Bose
on the counter, deafen
the crackling autumn.

Noodles in a pot boil over
into mush. There goes dinner,
just some chunks of stale bread
to toast and slather. There is a
trace of summer left in that last
ripe tomato, which I will slice,
salt, eat with a pinch of dill.

There are hurricanes offshore
and fires burning the Northwest.
The seasons turning can be
gentle or violent, but this year
in my woods, in my lucky state,
it is plain, simple, like my dinner
on a paper napkin.

Rust

the hue between brown and red reflected
again and again in the shimmer
of a speed boat's wake
rocking my rowboat
on this fall lake surrounded by forest.
On the palette of autumn, rust
dapples the hills,
age spots across the brilliant
ruby maples and yellow aspen.
Smoke from Canadian fires
dust the air turning sunset an orange rust,
the horizon oxidized.
The dusk smells of a dying campfire.
As the light of day diminishes
the trees quiet, the squirrels to their larder,
the birds dead-reckon their migration
sensing this year's erosion.
Rust the color of craving for summer
the trees desire for connection
through their roots and shared earth.
The dry leaves rub together with thirst,
wave with transience.
The crimson, the tarnished gold.
Rust the color of the woodland's corrosion.

Close to shore sheltering limbs overhead
are shingled with mottled leaves.
The sky is wearing camouflage.
The glint on the water is amethyst.
My boat crunches on the pebbled beach.

Rust flakes the white paint on the oarlocks
as I ship the oars and step out unsteadily
careful not to fall after my fall expedition.
Nothing to hold onto but my center of gravity
          my bare feet in cold water,
          my rusty joints straighten.

I feel the coming winter.

Lake George Loons

Listen to the loons in the harbor
they are wise in their weightless state
floating at sundown or morning,
I cannot tell the hour, the day,
as they bathe in the swirls and shadows.

The empty hours drag by, sideswipe
my sleepless state, taunt and call,
beckon me in, the water cool,
my pulse slow. An unease surfaces,
a headache, not cruel, loosely knit.

It feels like a laurel wreath has been
placed upon my crown, destiny born
between bedrock and stars. It is a victory
to wake each morning, write another page
in the annals of survival.

Fresh from revival, one step follows another,
one moment opens to the next, and I,
beneath an open sky, above the morning dew,
greet another day, as the loon does,
and follow its pace.

Late Spring, Lake George

During the late spring of the plague
the crows woke me at dawn
with their rude caw, caw, caws but
among the other early morning birdsong
I hear one above all the other call, here, here, here.

The bright green tips of the hemlock
fan above the rhododendron's lavender eruptions
on the edge of the wood, serene shade
a resting place.
My Shiloh where the Lord speaks.

Up here I include a boat's outboard among the sounds of
nature
since it is more welcome than the crash of the city
the jackhammers, car horns, truck alarms
the apocalyptic siren of an ambulance.
There is a reason why New York is the city that never sleeps.

Upstate, every day of late spring,
along with your first cup of coffee in the morning
comes the silent awareness of change.

Deep Deep Winter

In the depth of winter I finally reconcile
this is home, not a place to travel from
but to live in year round

I am used to the cold
icicles hang from the bitter eaves
my skin chaps from the wind
as I shovel the bawling snow

but always pumping in my veins
        summer
the lone owl hooting for a mate
hummingbirds zooming around the feeder

the heart knows hope like it knows the wind
it is what drives me as the shovel
glides along the deck

deep, deep winter
it is all memory

I am compelled to list the gratitudes of winter
        for the wool coat
        for the fireplace
        for the teapot
        for the quilt

I go deeper
    for the heart beating
    for the hand writing
    for the lungs breathing
    for the legs bending

It is late
Soon I will sleep
but in this darkened room
with a lit prayer candle
I think of my mother's home
a place to travel from
and to return
though briefly.

Not Spectacular

"Nature Trail" the sign said,
a vainglorious aspiration
as if dandelions are "organic greens."

It was the horse track to the icehouse
now a footpath of frozen winter mud
good enough to stretch my legs,
bathe in the trees' hibernation.

At the bottom of the hill,
the river and the icehouse ruins
a good place to sit and watch
a not so spectacular sunset
and read about a mystic
who heard God's music

and danced
unaware of herself.

I hunch in this clod
of my grudge-heavy body.
It's hard work to raise my head
lift my eyes to the sunset
sit with the dawning
awareness of gratitude
and listen.

Late Winter, 2020

Things are picking up
a new administration
I have been awakened
to the ice melt
my sense of defeat
has been dispelled
an alliance of unsettled
stars in the sky

I feel it just as I have felt
the comfort of winter
sleeping in
extravagant meals
blazing fires
it is coming—
a break in the weather

the crows confirm
my rickety notions
more cawing
more soaring and diving,
my sinuses unclogging
folks outside with jackets
unzipped, their lips
less chapped

a vista of shorn trees straightening
soon these trees will be tingling
birch, oak, elm—

woods, parks, yards
leafing up
stubs of brush
with tiny buds

even the rickety fence
will appear to have straightened
and I, immersed in winter,
await this transformation
in the quiet of my own body
as if justice and mercy
rain down from the stars.

Rising Groan

The trees were stripped
by the first hard winter wind.
The shriveled leaves blew like snow,
swirled in when I opened the door.

Snowstorm after ice storm
after the coldest day on record,
one gray day slogged into another
until we sloughed off January.

Winter-bedraggled February
dragged itself along on crutches.
March, a disappointment
to its entire family.

At Easter, warm words
emerge from my throat.
I babble about new life
as if it were the weather.

I'd have more to say
if I felt every death,
if I could retune the
rising groan into a song.

FRAILTIES

Watching the Turkey

The chilled air rises
I've eased from the bed
to squint at the amber sky

I hear a lone turkey
crunching leaves
in the yard

I peek through a door
which disturbs him
then a window

Every morning I hear him
on his hilly ascent from
roost to feeding

as predictable as a professor
in a tweed jacket or an
electrician with a lunch box

Does it matter
that I've lost the hearing
in my right ear?

I can still hear the turkey
when the world is quiet
as a temple

once the ear infection subsides
my hearing will return
I cling to this hope, a chokehold

The turkey trudges through
the underbrush, I stand aslant
to watch his progress

He leaves no tracks
which is another fear
I harbor

not just going deaf but
dying without leaving
a permanent mark

The deer have eaten the tulips
but there's a single daffodil
hanging limp in the dew

The turkey strides by, bows
to its yellow head amid
green shoots and dead leaves

I used to leave a porch light on
but now everyone who lives here
is sleeping

except me and the turkey
who are temporary residents
and of course

the permanent resident
of this household
Time

whistling through,
though I barely
hear her

Harbingers

Twelve, yes, an even dozen
of wild turkeys showed up
foraging, pecking in
the remains of the garden
at the end of the path
from my back door.

The larger ones have mottled grey heads
and a steady gaze.
The juveniles flap and fly-jump
when they see me,
scampering off to some just-safe
instinctual distance, but they don't leave.

They have been here for two days,
showed up after the rain
of a spectacular dawn lightning storm,
fall weather fell in behind it.

Harbingers of a Thanksgiving feast
or vultures over the end of my summer,
or both?
So much of life is like that,
either/or
a zero-sum game

but I'm a both/and guy
I accept the vultures
and the feast
as the harvest of the garden.

Meanwhile Poets Inside
Struggle with Verse

I walk the Cape May sand. Snow covers the dunes.
I breathe the air. The ocean crashes, wave after wave,
offers me the rhythm I seek, the heartbeat not yet broken,
the gulls overhead sing a poem, the song reminiscent of
ancient complaints, ancient warnings, the song repeated
as I cross the road to my room.

winter day, no storm
a solitary note
to be alive, hear!

Sing, Muse

Sing, Muse, you offkey nag
that's all you ever do.
Mute yourself.
When I should be watching Monk on Netflix
you whack me with your slipper
or wake me up in the middle of the night to scribble a line
or pull me up short in the middle of the street to tap out a note
on my phone.
Can't you leave me alone?

Dear Muse, remember, when poetry was a joy
when it was a puzzle we would do together
fitting the pieces, finding the right word
that meant two things,
something about the sea and a lightning strike,
some salty zinger.

This is one of those days
when you are more albatross than dove.
Can't we get back to cooing, gently,
making love, having fun with words.
That's what I want to do.

Sing if you must but soto voce.
Seduce me, be my lover.

Precious Light

I have tossed back the sheets
cracked the silence with a loud yawn
and there it is—light signing its name
across the sky—freely given
on numberless days, light!
or an echo of light, which sounds
improbable, day after night.

It wakes the creatures—birds to toads—
dusts their frailties and their faith
with falling leaves, and if any one thing
remains asleep, it clutches it with belief
in dawn, and the rising sun.

I see all of this, I have since childhood,
but I have never seen it so clearly as now,
my eyes clouded with age, my fingers knotted,
my breath just short of a wheeze, and yet I rise
with these aged eyes, and portion off the sky
just to see for one more day—light—precious light—
having survived midnight.

Seventy and Drawing Energy

My face in the heat of the Gulf Coast sun
doing Tai Chi near a banyan tree
this spring break is not about having fun
but accepting that I am elderly.

Across the yard is a companion tree
younger, its crown of branches full and green.
This one, a ghost web of grey twigs, weary
curled-up leaves and I stand in between.

I'm seventy and drawing energy
up from the earth and down from the sun
an ever-freshening grace blows through me
this spring break shows me my life is not done.

All These Years She Remembered

There was something on the radio this morning.
and I want very badly to tell you what I heard
but I can't remember now the story
or whether it was a man or a woman
telling the story.

It was a segment on NPR, that much I remember.
I was rolling over the railroad tracks, I believe,
on New Scotland Road South,
when I repeated to myself out loud
that I must remember this story.

It might have been a woman, an elderly
Jewish woman recounting her days
in the death camps, and since you are a history buff,
I thought you would want to know what she endured
and remembered, all these years she remembered.

Maybe I wasn't in the car.
Maybe I was still home, and the BBC reported
a recent accident on the Autobahn. You once said
they drive too fast on that damn road and why can't
those Germans drive at reasonable speeds like the rest of us.

I remember when you made that statement to me last summer.
You were sitting on the deck wearing your green polo shirt
and drinking iced tea with a sprig of mint. Your hair was
newly
trimmed, you had that newly-trimmed, little-boy look about
you,
the one I always said reminded me of your 6th-grade school
portrait,

the one where your hair is newly-trimmed and you are
wearing
a white shirt and tie, odd for a public school boy to be
wearing,
and then we spent the rest of the morning comparing public
vs.
Catholic school, and you razzed me about Catholic girls with
teased hair, and I told you about my first kiss on the school
bus.

Remember?

My Memory

My memory has gone to a nursing home
with no phone, or maybe to The Cloud
or up in smoke.

I don't remember the cakes
at any of my childhood birthdays.
The image in my mind of me
in a silver star-studded cowboy hat
with a six-gun on each hip
comes from a picture in an album.

A friend said to me, "Remember that
three-day trip we took to Cincinnati?"
No. I believe him when he says
we ate the best spaghetti with chili
but, I can't recall even a hint of spice
or one turn of the bus tire.

Once there was a funeral, the procession got stuck,
halted at the gate, turns out the fee hadn't been paid.
I remember being in line at Fort Lincoln for my Uncle Tony
but both my sisters correct me—it was Cedar Hill and Uncle Ernie.

I remember my bad memory
when I hear the news. Their facts
are like my memory's facts, indeterminate,
except theirs are for profit
and mine are just forfeited to time.

While You Are in Surgery

damaged from a fall
your left eye frail

        like a wasp
        or a sash on a wasp
        or petals fallen on the sash

your sight dimmed to scribbling

sometimes you feel crunching
        like coconut fibers
        or stale breadcrumbs
        or grit from a chicken yard

the doctor a deliverance
        your eye
        an onion peeled back
        it glistens

we plunge forward in hope
        the loving, honorable, bearable
        thing to do

we light candles
        If it be your will. . . . .

        blessings become pillars
        for the surgeon to lean against

a nagging disorder plagues us
        if you hadn't gone skiing
        if you hadn't turned 60
        if the first surgery had been successful

and if somehow I,
        drenched in the messiness
        of day after day
        could rise now

        take that scalpel
        whisper a prayer
        and slice.

Fear of Bridges

Driving up on freeway flyovers I feel like I'm going to fly off.
The periphery of every bridge wants to pull me over the side.
I cannot look wide, the only way across is a tight focus on the
trunk in front of me;
drive close and wear blinders. Each breath a prayer to blow
out the flare of panic.
When I'm out near the middle, my perineum tingles to tell me
there is nothing solid under me.
I wish I could look up at treetops and not at the road.

My world went flat after eye surgery;
my depth of field was gone.
Terror erupted the first time I drove
and the distant taillights in front of me were a wall.
Now my brain has adjusted
my eyes work better together.
I am conquering my fears.
The next thing you know I'll be on the high steel
of a nearly finished skyscraper
jabbering in Ojibway with my coworkers
about what we're going to have for lunch.

The Great Fire

Perhaps the earth, in fever, burns
just to be well.

The earth's pangs become lament,
the hush of trees weep in their own soil.

Perhaps, in neglecting signals,
we have missed the charred scent

until the brush burns over our own hill
down our ledge.

Like fugitives we run
from the planet's history

a collection of ignored truths
each truth filled to the brim

with feuds, each feud begun
by greed and greed itself

a door without memory,
a window without shutters.

We sweep ash into the urn,
eulogize those lost

in the Great Fire. We were there,
we decry, we were witness!

Prayer After the Fire

To the Anointed One we pray

for the wife driven out by wildfire,
her home gone, her husband
doesn't know where he is.
Bring glad tidings to her.

For those locked in shock
shaking their heads
and repeating "surreal."
Proclaim liberty to them.

For those whose past dissolved:
the poets and artists in exile,
the kids orphaned from school.
Recover their vision.

For the woman crushed
by the burden of her future
who says, "I'm sorry for my sadness."
Let the oppressed go free.

For the ones wasted with grief
who can't pass along heirlooms
to their children.
Anoint them with your spirit.

When any life crashes and burns
douse us with resilience,
the ability to persist, to start over.
Proclaim an acceptable year to restore.

Instructions on Flying

First choose well a jumping point
one with melody and symmetry
long stretches of field below
a wide site to circle

Relieve all debts, forgive all hurts
give thanks for every kindness
open your fragile arms to their
fullest, imagine them tufted

Listen for the wind's whistle
and the stroke of your inner timepiece
repeat your daily mantra or borrow
one from the ravens

Clutch the slender threads from
passing clouds, the tatters of rain
that fall from the mercurial sky,
lean into the wind, let go.

Free Climb or Free Fall

I wonder,
do they ever think about surrender?
Those fit men or women clinging
to the side of a sheer rock cliff
no safety harness, no rope
fingertips of one hand
pressed into an outcrop
thin steel-toed shoes wedged
into an invisible crevice
three extremities on point
and the other hand   reaching
          striving, testing
                    absorbed in absolute focus,
fear suppressed.

I imagine a free fall
the rush of the wind
that becomes silence
the acceleration into the void
the ultimate trust fall
not abandonment—
          those we love,
          we love more deeply,
          the good we pursued
          we bless and relinquish—
not abandonment but surrender.

There's no hard stop
only the ongoing fall
an infinite gyre
that, yes,
will pass through death
then be enfolded
into the flesh of The Infinite,
drawing us in since we began.

Thirteen Ways . . . a Mouse's Perspective

1. We nibble at the crumbs under the table.

2. Why do they scream? We are only hungry.

3. We nest in the garage, they set traps in the pantry.

4. We do not oink, nor bark, nor moo. We are silent but for the smallest squeak.

5. The cat—we are his plaything.

6. The owl screeches overhead, searching for a tidbit.

7. We laugh at the futility of the broom.

8. The small bag of chocolate chips on the shelf, a buzz.

9. We nuzzle in the nest after the feast.

10. Why do they jump on a chair? Why do they hide under a sheet?

11. The future is bleak, mouse-wise.

12. Sometimes I wander without caution.

13. Remember Fuzzy? Remember Pip?

Thirteen Questions for This Election

Why do I say obviously and
you say obviously and
we mean opposite things?

Why do you say
more walls
and I say vote for Walz
and we don't get along?

When the Trump Memorial Library
is built, will there be a shelf
for inelegant incoherence?

This is a poem that could shoot somebody
and still get elected a great poem.
Is this not the greatest election poem?

Who let the drunk street drummer
banging immigrant heads
against the street
into this election?
He's banging my head against the street
and yours, too.
Don't you notice?

Who normalized xenophobia
and called it patriotism?

Who shaped gay people into a wedge
and took a sledge to them
until we split?

Which Lady Liberty do you love,
the one by the golden door
or the one in your wallet?

Who will you vote for,
Daddy Warbucks
or Little Orphan Annie?

Do you remember Covid?
Why do I feel like the plague
is still with us?

When the time comes
and half of us don't get our way,
what will you unload?

When you die
and your life movie plays,
will the projector jam
on November 5th, 2024?

Nice When I Started

The day brought me here
though never in my life have I
loved this season, half-winter,
half spring, when it snows just
a bit, and that dusting remains
until noon, and then the temperature
winks at me, melts the flakes until
the trickle from the roof slows, then stops.

No buds yet, but the promise of buds.
Nothing green, but the chipmunks
are awake and the birds have received
the memo, and my tea is just the right combo
of sweet and bitter. The muffin is toasted and
buttered. But, within this reverie of seasonal
delight, You.

Everywhere. Headlines. Radio. TV.
Every damn conversation.
Your voice gives me the jimjams.

Your meathead politics.
Your screwball economics.
Your foghorn ego.

I've started a spreadsheet.
All the foul, mutinous garbage you spew.

The crew you have mutilated.
The party you have decimated.
You and your archfiends.

We were lulled, you know, for eight years.
I foresaw my retirement as restful,
contemplative, meditative, sanguine.
Instead, I'm marching, signing,
ringing doorbells, writing postcards,
avoiding conversations and members
of my own family, a lioness pouncing
on the newspaper, a madwoman
scanning the newsfeed, a narrator
of the end times.

You braggart.
You bamboozler.
You blunderer.
You bloated, brutish, bombastic bedsore.

You puppet.
You perpetrator.
You plunderer.
You pasty, profane, pitiful polecat.

You villain.
You violator.
You virus.
You vile, vain, venomous viper.

Calm down? You want me to calm down?
Might as well rip up the Constitution,
use it as kindling. I will not calm down.

I don't even know if my vote will be counted.
I don't even know if I'll make it to November,
or that you will refuse to leave.

Nice? There's no more nice. Nice stopped
on Nov. 8, 2016.

E Pluribus Unum

Oh my beloved
my parched beloved
dying of thirst
you drank the dirty water.
You live but
we have to live
with the plague
you've brought.

No, I don't hate you
my beloved
you want the best
for your chidren, too.

You leave me no choice.
Now I must find a community
where we help each other cope
and keep from being co-opted.

No Woke Words

Purged from government documents
hundreds of words that to me seem safe
or at least void of controversy—
        gender, women, breastfeed—
        disability, equity, identity—
        and so many other "ity" words.

But for some reason, not malignant narcissist, nor
        security leak
        willful blindness
        measles outbreak
        insubordination
        inhumanity
        incomprehensible
        indefensible

Nor   fraud
        treason
        money laundering
        lying under oath
        sexual assault
        witness tampering
        forgery
        racketeering
        corruption
        larceny
        felony
        blackmail
        coercion

long-tungu'd babbling gossip
beetle-headed flop-eared knave!

I'm sorry, I've lost my train of thought. . . . .

The point, and academics might agree,
that words—by themselves—
are no more than a cudgel
to knock the sense into
or out of a sentence.

They can be a doorway
to miscommunication and confusion,
a bottleneck of burdensome letters
chained together, disguised as
revelations from underaged,
inexperienced voices
meandering in our skulls,
creating an attic filled with
yellowing newspapers,
with headlines declaring
World War II is Over!
JFK Assassinated!
President Nicked in His Right Ear!

Rage and Resist

Isaiah, Jeremiah, Amos,
Malachi and John the Baptist
Rage with me at this new Herod,
this builder of golden temples.

Rage against our common well
poisoned by hate, distilled from fear.
The billionaires will drink bottled water
but the immigrant mother
the Muslim brother
the handicapped boy
are gut-sick
profaned.

Rage until your nerve-wracked heart
turns to more durable stuff.

Rage with me Bonhoeffer
and bring your pen, louder than a bomb.
Rage with me Ghandi and King
and bring your iron love
Rage with me Desmond Tutu
and show me how you stared down the beast.

Rage against the hate.
Purge it with a very loud love.
One that sings and cracks glass ceilings.
A love so strong
it unbends the crooked cross of Hitler.

Resist any new normal
where the bully pulpit
is now the bully's throne.
Where a migrant worker sleeping in a bus station
is taunted and beaten.
Where a Latina on a subway platform is told,
"I can't wait until I can rape you
and throw you over the wall."
Where a gay man is beaten bloody for being himself.
Where a ten-year-old girl's privates are groped
by a boy in her class who says,
"If the President can do it, so can I."

Resist any new normal
where the golden rule is:
Hate your neighbor as you hate yourself.

About the Authors

Mimi Moriarty lives in a log home on an escarpment overlooking the Hudson Valley. She has authored three poetry chapbooks: *Sibling Revery* (co-authored with her brother, Frank Desiderio), *War Psalm* (Finishing Line Press), and *Crows Calling* (Foothills Publications). She holds an MFA in Creative Writing from Goddard College, Plainfield, VT, and has numerous poems, stories, and articles in anthologies, magazines, and newspapers throughout the country.

Frank Desiderio produces two video poems in the key of spirituality each week on his Substack, *Holy Poetry.* He authored the book *Can You Let Go of a Grudge (*Paulist Press, 2014). His poems appear in many journals, including *Spring Hill Review, Windhover, Amethyst Review, America, Presence, Gnashing Teeth's 'zine, Little Old Lady Comedy, Eunoia Review, Thin Places and Sacred Space,* and *Moving Image by Poetry Inspired by Film.* He and his sister, Mimi Moriarty, authored the chapbook *Sibling Revery* (Finishing Line Press). Currently, he lives in Manhattan on Lenape homelands and finds joy in his family, poetry and Tai Chi.

Website:
holipoetry.substack.com

www.ingramcontent.com/pod-product-compliance
Lightning Source LLC
LaVergne TN
LVHW090530110826
845146LV00003B/1050

* 9 7 9 8 9 0 1 4 6 9 1 5 6 *